Show Me Your GBER

How Are You Doing?

By
Gaylen K. Bunker

BusinessAllStars, Salt Lake City, Utah 84109

Table of Contents

Acknowledgements

I want to express appreciation for the generous contributions made by my wife, Diane, who has read and reread the manuscript many times and given extremely valuable input. I also want to thank her for a wonderful evening on the Seine.

Gaylen K. Bunker

Introduction

Warren Buffett said: "It is easier to entertain than to educate." This book is an effort to teach financial concepts in such a way that students of business will not only understand them, but find them comfortably wrapped in an interesting story.

Let me assure you that all of the characters in this little book are fictional and bear no resemblance to anyone that I know, not even me.

Gaylen K. Bunker

A Flight to Paris

He walked slowly toward the boarding area and glanced at his watch. He still had time before the first call to board. He spotted a free seat a few rows away in the morass of waiting passengers lounging in the connected chairs and worked his way to it. He sat down, placed his carry-on between his feet and fumbled with the book he had just purchased at the gift shop and his leather bound zippered loose-leaf.

Taking a deep breath he glanced out the window to see if his plane was at the gate and as he did he caught sight of a smartly dressed woman in her mid thirties seated a few places down and across from him. She had long raven hair that fell over a soft black light-weight turtle-neck sweater. Her slacks neatly conformed to a thin and trim figure. She was obviously a confident woman of some means.

Returning his focus to his book, he overheard the attendant announce that first class passengers were boarding. He stood, gathered his things and began to make his way toward the gate. He produced his ticket, had it scanned and proceeded toward the door. Once inside the plane he found his seat number, stowed his bag in the overhead compartment and sat down. As he did, the woman he had noticed in the terminal was suddenly standing to his side reaching up and placing a bag in the overhead compartment next to his.

"Excuse me; I think that is my seat, by the window," she motioned across him.

He stood up, slid to the side, and let her pass---to the seat next to his. Being a people watcher at heart, his attention was drawn away from the woman and to the boarding passengers. They filed in one after another, passed him and were lost somewhere behind him in the plane. He couldn't help feeling thankful that he was in first class where he had a little leg room and not crunched between restrictive barriers on all sides. Eventually, the attendant closed the door and everyone began to settle in.

The plane made a smooth take-off, gained altitude and then leveled off. As it did he inspected his book: front cover, back cover, title page, and introduction---everything. Then he went to page one and began to lose himself in the journey the book offered. He didn't pay much attention to the woman in the seat next to him until he became aware that she seemed to be looking at the loose-leaf that was resting on his lap. As he turned in her direction, she glanced up and then away to the window. He looked down to see the bold lettering emblazoned on the cover of his loose-leaf: "Show Me Your GBER."

He didn't know whether to say anything or not. It was always a question. Do you open the door of conversation with the passenger in the next seat and risk being bluntly put off and then suffering a socially awkward situation for the next several hours? On the other hand, his business was GBER and this seemed to be a natural lead in. The next time she glanced around, he spoke up: "Hello, are you going to Paris on business?" It was a lame question, but it began the conversation.

"Yes, are you?"

"As a matter of fact I am. I'm presenting a training session to a few European executives on the value of GBER."

"I noticed your leading line---'Show me Your GBER. It sounds rather suggestive."

"It is meant to get people's attention."

"Do I dare ask what a GBER is?" she queried somewhat reluctantly.

"Before I answer that, do you mind if I ask you a few questions?"

"You can try," she replied guardedly.

"What kind of business are you in?"

"I own a boutique that sells high-end women's apparel."

"How is business?"

"We have been open for about three years and I'm proud to say we are in the black."

"That's great. Is this a buying trip?"

"Are you sure you're not with the IRS?"

"I promise. It is just that I like to assess the frame of reference relative to our common interest in business. GBER is a global metric that tells you how your business is really doing."

"What do you mean by 'really doing'? I told you I'm in the black, covering all my costs and making a little extra."

"How much background do you have in financial analysis?"

"I have a bachelors degree in marketing, if that's what you're wondering."

"I would assume you had to take basic courses in economics, accounting and finance as a part of your degree program?"

"There were a few along the way. I did pretty well in them, but probably couldn't tell you right now much of anything that was covered."

"I see: a classic case of bulimic learning. You fattened up during the course and then purged on the final."

She shrugged her shoulders. "Hey, I'm a marketing person, and now a small business owner who has a major debt and tons of optimism."

"Perhaps you shouldn't show me your GBER. I would hate to take the wind out of your sails," he offered reluctantly.

"Now you do have my interest. How can GBER compromise my enthusiasm?"

"Oh, it wouldn't, but it might give you a different perspective." He normally charged clients a major fee for continuing past this point, but she was very interesting to him on many levels. "Do you drive a car?"

"Yes."

"GBER is not the car, the road, the driver, or the journey. It is much like the speedometer that can tell you critical data about your driving experience, but only if you choose to employ it. Some people think financial analysis is a magical tool that can cure what ails the business. It simply gives you information. The rest is up to you. It's much like college: it gives you tools, a degree, and even access to employment, but once on the job, the actual performance is what you make of it."

"Got it," she snapped.

"Let me see if you recall any financial terms from your undergraduate program. Do you remember NOPAT, WACC, Invested Capital, Break-Even Analysis, Excess Earnings, Residual Income, or EVA?" he queried.

"Only vaguely, but remember, I was a marketing major."

"Yes, but now you are a business owner."

"True," she confessed. "Go on."

"To do this right, I would need to know a lot more about your business---financially."

She hesitated and he could tell she was weighing the benefit versus cost of sharing more intimate details of her business. Finally, she said, "I was about to review my past year's performance during the flight. I have a set of financials here in my carry-on." She motioned to an executive bag at her feet. She reached down and pulled a folder from the bag. As she did, he raised his tray from its hiding place and secured it in front of him as his working table.

She held the folder in her hand as she studied him for a long moment and then set it down on his tray. He wondered to himself if this was the first step toward---surrendering to him. There seemed to be a personal connection between them that he did not exactly understand, and couldn't help but wonder if she felt it too.

An Intimate Portrait

He opened the folder and peered at the data. "This is quite an operation. You had total revenue of about $5 million last year, cost of goods sold of $2 million and a bottom line of a hundred thousand. Not bad, that is about a two percent net income." He flipped through the supporting pages. "It looks like you have quarterly data here also. Are these numbers on a cash or accrual basis?"

"I think my accountant said he converts them to quasi-accrual at the end of each reporting period---whatever that means."

"A lot of smaller companies record transactions as they pay or receive cash. Like a check book. These cash flows can swing wildly from one quarter to the next, depending on how people feel about paying their bills, both coming and going. This can result in some quarters looking absolutely wonderful and others a disaster. Accrual accounting helps to smooth things out and reflect a matching of revenues earned and the expenses that generated those revenues. It is a better way. I'm glad your accountant does this for you."

"He seems pretty thorough," she admitted.

"Well, the first step is to convert Net Income into 'Net Operating Profit After Taxes' or what is commonly called NOPAT. Normally, to do a full blown analysis we would make several adjustments, but for our purposes we will do a quick and dirty."

"Why do we want NOPAT as you call it?"

"There are several expenses that make up the Net Income that are not a part of NOPAT. One of these is interest expense. It is subtracted from Revenue as an operating cost when in fact it is a financing cost."

"What's the difference?"

"When you started your business did you have to buy a lot of stuff? You know, I mean hard assets."

"Yes, I had to have my location remodeled to my specifications. Talk about a conversion, I had to transform a failed toy store into a very exclusive women's boutique. That was not easy. In addition to moving walls, painting, electrical and plumbing I had to purchase specialized fixtures and furniture."

"So you invested in assets that should last for several years before they needed to be replaced?"

"That's right," she agreed as she reached over, shuffled through the papers and pointed out the property, plant and equipment under the heading fixed assets listed on the balance sheet.

"There, it cost me close to a million dollars to get started."

"Part came from my personal assets, part from family, and the rest from a small business loan. I put up the original half million, but I've had to go to my family for an additional $200,000 to cover what my accountant calls working capital."

"I'm sure the interest expense or financing cost is related to that loan?" he offered.

"That's right," she countered.

"I'm going to jot a few of your numbers on this yellow pad so I can do some figuring. I'll only show the numbers in thousands, which means I'll drop the three digits at the end of each number just for ease in working with them."

"There," he said with pride as he copied the balance sheet and created a document he could make notes on. "If I were an artist I couldn't have sketched a better picture of you, but not just a portrait in a studio. This is a picture that shows your physical appearance and your character as well. It tells me your strengths and weaknesses, your ability to keep your commitments, and who can exercise power over you. It tells me your age, if you trust other people and if they trust you. I know more about you by looking at this statement than if I were to see you naked in your bath."

Balance Sheet (Year end)　　Portrait

Cash & Cash Equivalents	150	OC
Accounts Receivable	325	
Inventory	300	
Other Current Assets	150	
Current Assets	925	
Property, Plant & Equip	1,000	IC
Accumulated Deprec	(375)	
Total Assets	1,550	

Accounts Payable	250	OC
Other Current Liabilities	50	
Current Liabilities	300	
Notes Payable	500	
Total Debt	800	FC
Common Stock	700	
Retained Earnings	50	
Total Liab & Equity	1,550	

"You think so, do you?" she said with skepticism and a smirk. "What do you think, am I decent or not?"

"You look pretty good, not great, but pretty good." He could sense that her physical beauty, the way she carried herself and the clothing she wore intimidated most people. Perhaps she found it refreshing to find someone who didn't acquiesce to her powers or maybe she saw him as a challenge yet to be conquered. Of course he was interested in her and flattered that she would trust him enough to share the numbers, but he had no intention of giving her the upper hand.

"Tell me, who has power over me?" she asked. She did not even flinch concerning the naked comment, but the issue of control obviously touched a nerve.

I Believe in You

"On the asset side you have $325,000 of uncollected accounts receivable. These are customers that have power because they did not pay in cash, but demanded credit and you gave it to them. As a matter of fact, if I divide your $5,000,000 annual revenue by 365 days, you generate about $13,700 per day in sales.

$$\frac{\$\ 5,000,000}{365} = \$\ 13,700$$

"If I divide the $325,000 in accounts receivable by your sales per day, we just calculated, you have about 24 days of sales that are uncollected at any one time."

$$\frac{\$\ 325,000}{\$\ 13,700} = 24\ days$$

"Putting it another way, it takes you a little over three and a half weeks to collect after a sale is made."

"Do you think that's good or bad?"

"It seems high to me for a retail shop where most people pay with a credit card, which is almost like cash. I think you have some very high end women that like to carry an account with you."

"That's exactly how it is. I remember the day the president of the women's guild came in. She wanted to purchase a stunning blue ensemble I brought back from Milan. It wasn't even a question of whether or not she could afford it. She wanted to set up a revolving account and charge it. I saw this as a way to capture even more of her business and establish a permanent customer. It was one of the best decisions I ever made, because it led to an explosion of business from the women's guild."

"I would suspect you have very few accounts that are uncollected and have to be written off?"

"There are a few, but not many. We are very selective and our clients know it. This wasn't a way of surrendering power, but rather of forming a partnership with the powerful."

The Discount Shop
"You also have $300,000 in inventory which must be sold in the near future. If I check the numbers and divide $2,000,000 Cost of Goods Sold by 365 days, I calculate that inventory cost you about $5,500 per day.

$$\frac{\$\ 2,000,000}{365} = \$\ 5,500$$

"Dividing the $300,000 inventory by the $5,500 in the cost of daily sales indicates that an item will remain on the racks for almost 55 days before it goes out the door."

$$\frac{\$ \ 300{,}000}{\$ \ 5{,}500} = 55 \ days$$

"That is nearly two months. I'm not a retail expert and certainly not when it comes to women's fashion, but is that reasonable?"

"I never calculated that number, but have a general sense that it is correct," she confirmed.

"Once again your customers have the power to make or break you. If they buy, you move inventory and it's not a problem. If they don't, you will have to slash prices or even write some things off. I would say your customers have a significant amount of power over you."

"You make it sound as though my customers are tyrants and I'm their slave. I have a great reputation and most of my customers feel it is a real privilege to purchase something from my shop. I'm not so sure I agree with your assessment."

"I would suspect one of the most critical aspects of your business is the buying trip," he queried.

"You're absolutely right. I'm the shop and the shop is me. What I buy is what we sell and my clients count on my judgment and expertise. I don't have a lot of ability with the figures in financial statements, but I have tremendous talent in knowing what to put on the figures of my clients."

"What becomes of clothing that does not sell? Do you have some process for dealing with older items that remain on the racks?"

"Because we don't sell in bulk and most of our pieces are unique I don't feel compelled to move them out if they don't sell in the requisite time frame. If an item remains on the racks longer than I think it should, I must make a decision. I've only recently set up a separate shop where I offer items at prices below full retail. That has been a gamble for me, because I don't want to compromise my brand and send the wrong message. It is a bare bones rented space about a block from my main location."

She continued, "It is amazing to see how many women want to wear high-end apparel on a budget. It is opening up a whole new market where I'm beginning to buy items that go straight to that shop. I really feel that I'm controlling that market, it is not controlling me." She paused and then added, "Is that all you've got?"

Power Trio

"No, there's more. The two operating assets we just discussed, accounts receivable and inventory, plus one of your operating liabilities, accounts payable, I refer to as the power trio. They provide the financial power to your business; the operating energy, so to speak."

Cash & Cash Equivalents	150	
Accounts Receivable	325	OC
Inventory	300	
Other Current Assets	150	
Current Assets	925	

Accounts Payable	250	OC
Other Current Liabilities	50	
Current Liabilities	300	

He pointed to a spot further down on the balance sheet. "You have $250,000 of outstanding accounts payable. This represents claims on your business by vendors who have extended credit to you when you purchased inventory from them. I divided accounts receivable by revenue per day because those numbers were both at cost plus mark-up. I use cost of goods sold per day when analyzing inventory and accounts payable because they are carried at cost, without any mark-up added."

16

"We just calculated the cost of your daily sales as $5,500. If I divide that number into the $250,000 in accounts payable it tells me that from the time you receive your goods it takes you about 45 days to pay the vendors."

$$\frac{\$\ 250,000}{\$\ 5,500} = 45\ days$$

"That is a month and a half. Until you pay the bills these vendors have a direct claim on your business. It does show they have great faith in you, but if they ever decided to stop extending credit, you would be in a world of hurt."

"Everything you have mentioned so far, I'm totally aware of. You see, because credit is given and received it is not that they have power over me; it is more a validation of my superior ability to run a business. They want to move product and they trust me. The fact that I can extend payment to 45 days is more a measure of the power I have and not the other way around."

"I like your optimism. You must be a cup half full kind of person."

"You don't succeed in business without confidence and faith in yourself. Besides, if what you calculate is correct and it takes 55 days to sell an item, then paying in 45 days is nearly matching the outflow of goods with the outflow of payment on those goods. I say that is good business." She paused a moment.

"Anyone else you think has power over me?"

He had the sense their discussion was turning into a duel or a fencing match at thirty thousand feet in the air. He would attack and she would defend and then counter attack. She seemed to enjoy the challenge, and besides, all the attention was on her and she appeared to love it.

The Gamblers

His finger moved to the bottom of the balance sheet he had fashioned:

Notes Payable	500	
Total Debt	800	FC
Common Stock	700	
Retained Earnings	50	

"Two other areas: Your Notes Payable of $500,000 and the $200,000 of the Common Stock that was invested by people, other than yourself, that is part of the $700,000 shown on the balance sheet. Those who lent you money and those who invested in your company, both groups have gambled on you, and the latter are willing to risk receiving nothing in return. The Notes Payable bunch---they demand interest and principle on a very rigid schedule and if those payments are missed, you are out of business."

"Let me just say there is a lot of history behind those numbers. You can't imagine what I had to go through to get that loan. The money from my family---that is a completely different story."

Borrowed Money

"Before I ever opened my boutique, I had been planning that event for years. In high school, a local department store selected a group of girls from my school to be on a special fashion board. I was selected and worked closely with buyers at the store. I'll never forget our discussions about fabrics, colors, trends, and markets. I was hooked.

"That year, for my prom dress, I personally selected this incredible dark blue number from the store and felt like an absolute knock-out at the dance. I wanted every other girl to have that same thrill that I experienced.

"After high school, I worked my way through college part time for the store, in the backroom stocking all the goods, then as an assistant on the floor during evenings and weekends and finally, as a full commission sales associate in my senior year.

"After college I went to New York and enrolled in a graduate program in fashion merchandising. I never finished the program because I landed a job at an exclusive boutique. From that point on, I worked my tail off and saved every dime I could with the idea that someday I would have my own shop.

"I realized that I had an eye, or what you might call a gift, for picking what really sold and matched current trends. I was an information bloodhound, reading every fashion magazine, association and trade publication, and article from any source that related to the industry and trends. At first I would travel with the main buyer and assist on selections. The items I chose were almost always the best movers at the store. Eventually, I was made the lead buyer for some of the markets.

"When I finally could scrounge half a million from all savings, personal resources, credit cards, a second mortgage and whatever, I decided to go out on my own. That is when the fun began.

"I looked at various other sources of financing, and what an education that was. I had to go through a checklist like you can't believe. Well, you probably can. My business plan had to address the business purpose, mission, strategy, markets, products, pricing, competition, suppliers, trademarks and brands."

"They wanted to know all about my background: what skills and abilities I would bring to the table. They wanted to know who else was involved and what their backgrounds were; had they worked together before and what was the organizational structure. That was all before we got into the numbers.

"My accountant helped me with an estimate of what funds we would need and how they would be used. We had to forecast revenues for the next five years and a detailed cash flow projection, by month for the first three years. It was amazing."

He interjected, "I don't think that is unusual. They are gambling their money on you."

"I looked at all the various sources of financing. Venture Capitalists wanted over 50% control of the business and a 75% return each year. Then they would sell off the business after three to five years. I found an Angel Investor, but they wanted 25 and 25: twenty-five percent equity ownership and a 25% return each year. Finally, a bank agreed to a loan through the Small Business Administration. No equity ownership was involved, but a very strict repayment plan was required."

"After I put up my money and the bank's money I launched the business. That is when I found out how to rapidly expand the business by extending credit to the women from the guild. It was going to take even more money, but I was tapped out."

Other Equity

"Someone told me another option was FFF or Family, Friends, and Fools. I have a rich Uncle Walter who I thought might help. When I talked to him it was probably one of the most depressing moments in my family history. He flatly said no."

"When I got home that night I got a call from Aunt Jenny, Walter's wife. She was not there when I talked with Uncle Walter, but when she heard about what I wanted she pretty well told Walter where to put it. Now, I always thought I was Walter's favorite and Jenny was a little distant, but you can never tell. She told me to come back the next day and she would have a check waiting with no strings attached. Wow!"

"I look at these sources of financing not as an extension of power over me, but as a validation of who I am." Then pointing to the page she asked, "What are these things on the side---OC, IC, and FC?"

"Accountants like to categorize groups of items on the balance sheet as Operating, Investing, or Financing Capital. It is just too bad that financial analysts haven't caught up to this. It would be a lot easier if the two fields were more integrated."

He wondered if he had been too aggressive with the power thing. She was a proud woman and he had taken some pretty negative shots at her, but he was sure she was sufficiently thick skinned to get where she was. "Let's move on to the Income Statement," he said.

Not Your Dad's Net Income

"The decision regarding how much to borrow is completely independent from the ongoing operations of the business. If you financed the whole business from your own savings, there would be no debt and no interest expense. If you borrowed the whole amount, then the interest expense would be much larger. The point being: financing decisions are generally very different from ongoing operating decisions---salaries, rent, utilities, insurance, supplies, advertising, and such."

"Okay."

She leaned in close to look at the numbers and he took a deep breath, savoring a gentle fragrance that seemed to surround her. As he paused she sensed the delay and leaned back expecting him to continue the explanation.

He looked down at the pages, turned back to the income statement and pointed to the interest expense. "If we subtract the $60,000 of interest expense from the other expenses then the bottom line will increase by that amount. But not only that: If we didn't have the interest expense, then income taxes would be much higher. We say that interest expense provides a tax break."

"That's good isn't it?"

"Sure, but it also means that your true cost for interest expense is not the $60,000. Let me see." He quickly crunched some numbers in his head. "Taxes were $33,000, so if I add that back to the Net Income of $100,000, the before tax amount would be $133,000."

$$\$ 100,000 \quad + \quad \$ 33,000 \quad = \quad \$ 133,000$$

"It looks like the tax rate is about 25%, or $33,000 taxes on $133,000 of before-tax income."

$$\frac{\$ \quad 33,000}{\$ \quad 133,000} \quad = \quad 25.0\%$$

"If I increase the before-tax amount by the interest expense that is no longer a part of the income statement, then it will be $133,000 plus $60,000 or $193,000. Twenty-five percent tax on that amount would be about $48,000, so you get a $15,000 tax break because of having interest expense."

"If you take out the interest expense, which increases the before tax amount and apply the same tax rate to the new total?

$$\$ 193,000 \quad \times \quad 25\% \quad = \quad \$ 48,000$$

Then, $193,000 minus $48,000 would leave $145,000."

She shook her head, "You lost me."

Before			After
Revenue	$5,000	$5,000	Revenue
Oper Exp	($4,682)	($4,682)	Oper Exp
Depr. Exp	($125)	($125)	Depr Exp
EBIT	193	193	EBIT
Int Exp	($60)		
EBT	133	193	EBT
Taxes	($33)	($48)	Taxes
Net Inc	$100	$145	NOPAT

He pointed to the figures on his newly reconfigured income statement. "Instead of $100,000 of Net Income, we now have $145,000 NOPAT or Net Operating Profit After-Taxes. That is because we took out interest expense of $60,000 and income taxes of $15,000."

"So we don't use interest expense and the related taxes at all?"

"We are going to use them, but later."

Just then the attendant came by offering some refreshment and the discussion about GBER was put on hold. They made small talk for a while about airline service and the advantages of first class as they ate. She had the appearance of someone very confident that could put you in your place very quickly, but there seemed to be an increasing connection between them that made talking to her very exciting. All the signals that she sent were sincere, and so he went with it.

Suddenly she turned to him and said, "So why do we want NOPAT?"

"We can't use Net Income because interest expense is a financing cost, but has been incorporated in the Income Statement as if it were an operating cost. So by taking interest expense and the related tax break out of the Income Statement we are left with only the operating revenues and expenses that results in NOPAT instead of Net Income."

"What comes next?" she pressed.

A Little Too Personal

"The next thing we need to do is find out what it costs you to finance your company."

"Well, that seems very simple. The interest expense is $60,000."

"That is the cost to finance the debt or what you borrowed. There is still the cost of equity." He opened the financial statements to the balance sheet and pointed to the liabilities and equity. "Some of these liabilities have no cost associated with them, such as Accounts Payable and Other Accruals. So if we subtract those from the total, everything that is left has a cost."

She looked at the numbers. "There is the half a million I borrowed and the rest of the stuff is what my family and I put up, plus some profits my accountant calls retained earnings."

Notes Payable	500	
Total Debt	800	FC
Common Stock	700	
Retained Earnings	50	

"That's right, a half million in debt and the $750,000 in equity."

"But the equity doesn't cost me anything."

"On the contrary, it costs you a great deal, much more that the $60,000 interest expense on the half million. The interest cost is about 12%, excluding the tax benefit."

$$\frac{\$ \ 60,000}{\$ \ 500,000} = 12.0\%$$

"If I count that $15,000 in tax savings against the interest expense, then the true cost is $45,000 divided by $500,000 or about 9%."

$$\frac{\$ \ 45,000}{\$ \ 500,000} = 9.0\%$$

What's Your Salary?

"Now I'm going to assume you pay yourself a pretty decent salary," he continued.

Suddenly she became a little cooler. It appeared that the mention of her salary and perks were a sensitive issue.

He recovered quickly. "You don't need to tell me exactly what you earn, but I'm going to make some theoretical assumptions. Let's say you pay yourself about $400,000 a year."

Before she could say anything he interjected. "Just go with me on this."

"Okay," she said skeptically.

"Suppose for some reason you could not work directly at the boutique, what would you pay a manager to come in and handle things?"

"Well, assume I was taking $400,000 per year," she said with some exaggeration. "You know I not only manage the place, I do all the buying and am basically responsible for everything."

"What if you hired a manager to run the day-to-day and another person to do the buying, what would you pay them?"

"I might pay them $100,000 each," she concluded.

"That's $200,000 compared to the $400,000 you are taking. The difference of $200,000 is really a dividend or a return on your equity investment as an owner."

"Are you saying the salaries expense on my income statement is wrong? That they are overstated by $200,000?"

"Not exactly, I'm just saying your salary as the owner has two parts. One part is the payment for your management ability and buying expertise. The other part is compensation for being the owner that you would not normally pay to hired employees."

	Before		
Revenue	$5,000	$5,000	Revenue
Oper Exp	($4,682)	($4,482)	Oper Exp
Depr. Exp	($125)	($125)	Depr Exp
EBIT	193	393	EBIT
Int Exp	($60)		
EBT	133	393	EBT
Taxes	($33)	($98)	Taxes
Net Inc	$100	$295	NOPAT

"This is much like the interest expense. It is financing cost embedded in the operating expenses of the company, but instead of cost paid to those who lent you money, it goes to those who invested in the equity. It also needs to be adjusted for taxes. The taxes on $200,000 would be $50,000 or 25% of it."

$$\$ 200,000 \times 25\% = \$ 50,000$$

We subtract that to end up with a net $150,000.

$$\$ 200,000 - \$50,000 = \$ 150,000$$

She clarified, "What you're saying is the $150,000 after-tax excessive salary that I received is a return on my equity investment and is a financing cost to the company, not an operating cost. But it does nothing for Aunt Jenny and Uncle Walter."

"That's right. Technically they should be receiving a similar return on their investment. Because they don't, we average the return on the total equity."

"If we look at the newly adjusted NOPAT of $295,000 we find three things there: $100,000 of original Net Income, $150,000 of net dividends to equity holders and $45,000 of net interest expense. The first two belong to the equity investors, it's just that $100,000 is reinvested back into the company on the equity holder's behalf and the $150,000 is paid out as a dividend."

"When the dividend is divided by the equity we get $150,000 over $750,000 which results in a 20% return or what is called a dividend yield."

$$\frac{\$\ 150{,}000}{\$\ 750{,}000} = 20.0\%$$

"But that is not the only return investors expect. Did you mention how fast your company is growing from year to year?"

"I'm not sure if I did, but we grew by 20% this last year and I expect that kind of growth to continue in each of the next several years," she offered.

"When someone invests in something they normally expect two kinds of returns. If you were to purchase a share of Nordstrom stock and it cost $50 today, what would be your expectations?"

"What do you mean my expectations?"

"There are a lot of reasons you may want to own such stock, but for most investors they are hoping the stock will pay a dividend. Now suppose that Nordstrom paid a $1.00 dividend for every share of stock and so you received your $1.00 in the mail. As we just calculated that would be $1.00 divided by $50.00 or a 2% dividend yield.

$$\frac{\$\ 1.00}{\$\ 50.00} = 2.0\%$$

You earned 2% on your investment. Is that all you expect?" he pressed.

"No I would hope the stock price would go up and so I could make money by the appreciation of the stock when I sold it."

"That is exactly right. So in addition to the dividend yield of 2% you would also expect some kind of growth in the stock itself. If

Nordstrom's revenue and earnings were growing at 10% each year, wouldn't you as the investor hope that would be passed along to you? In other words, you would hope the price of the stock would also go up by 10% each year so that after one year of holding the stock you could sell it for $55."

$$\$\,50.00 \quad \times \quad 1.10\% \quad = \quad \$\,55.00$$

"Sure," she admitted.

"Let's return to your company. We said that your company had a dividend yield of 20% and you indicated that your company expected to grow by another 20% each year. If we added those two together we would find that a normal investor would expect a 40% return on their investment in your company."

$$20.0\% \quad + \quad 20.0\% \quad = \quad 40.0\%$$

"Wow, I guess I never thought to put it into those types of terms. I wonder if my uncle and aunt know about this?" she mused.

"We should normally project this over a long time frame, but my quick and dirty approach has given us a number that is probably in the ball park."

"You are beginning to know a lot more about me personally than I expected. Are you sure GBER isn't a term for something we shouldn't be discussing as almost total strangers?"

"It is nothing of a personally intimate nature, but my intent is to completely undress your company and get to the real figures."

She studied him for a long moment and then said, "I can handle it. Where do we go from here?"

Take a Whack at That

"We need to combine the various parts of financing cost into a single measure we will call the Weighted Average Cost of Capital. You have $500,000 of debt and $750,000 of equity for a total of $1,250,000. So of the total, 40% is debt and 60% is equity---right?"

"Let's see---$500,000 divided by $1,250,000 is 40% and $750,000 divided by $1,250,000 is 60%. Okay, I'm with you," she agreed.

$$\frac{\$\ 500{,}000}{\$\ 1{,}250{,}000} = 40.0\%$$

$$\frac{\$\ 750{,}000}{\$\ 1{,}250{,}000} = 60.0\%$$

"Remember we said the debt costs 9% after taxes and the equity costs 40%."

"Yes."

"If we multiply the weight of debt times the after-tax cost of debt we get a component cost of 3.6%. Then if we multiply the weight of equity times the cost of equity we get a component cost of 19.8%. Adding these two components together we get a weighted average cost of 27.6%. That is what it costs your company for the financing it maintains."

	Weight	Cost	component
Debt	40.00%	9%	3.60%
Equity	60.00%	40%	24.00%
Fin Cap	100%		27.60%

"Why do I want to know that?" she wondered.

"Every company needs financing to operate and pay for expansion. It is critical that the company understand what the cost of their combined financing is when it comes to evaluating operating and growth decisions. If the return you generate from operating the business is not greater than the cost to finance the operations, then you should rethink the decision. It offers a hurdle or required return for most decisions."

"There is something about you I find very intriguing. I'm totally aware of the people around me and when you first checked me out at the terminal, my initial impression was that you were a frumpy professor type who had no business looking in my direction. Then when I found that we were seated next to each other I was hoping you wouldn't attempt to talk to me.

Do you know what it was about you that intrigued me?"

Taken aback, he wondered what was coming next.

"It was your eyes and that stupid title: 'Show Me Your GBER.' The more we've talked, the more I've gained respect for you. Now don't take this wrong, but most people in my world are extremely superficial and caught up in outward appearances. That's just the world I work in. You are surprisingly deep and refreshing, in a number-crunching kind of way."

"I don't quite know what to say." He was taken aback by the direct evaluation. "Where do we go from here?"

"You finish telling about this GBER thing, and what I'm trying to say is that you are okay, I like you."

He took a deep breath. His mind was racing. He really didn't care what she thought of him, he had enough confidence to take whatever she said with a grain of salt. He had correctly assessed her to begin with. She was a power woman with a great figure and clothes to match, but damn it, he liked her too. "Okay, let us recap. What is NOPAT?"

"It is the Net Operating Profit After Taxes for the year, excluding interest expense, hidden dividends to owners and the related tax savings on each."

"How much is yours?"

"My NOPAT is $295,000."

"Excellent. What is Financing Capital?"

"It is the moneys lent to the company or invested in the company that have an associated cost in either interest expense, dividends or expected growth."

"How much is yours?"

She looked through her notes. "It is $1,250,000."

"What is the cost of debt?" he continued.

"It is interest expense less the tax savings divided by the debt outstanding."

"And your cost is?"

"My cost of debt is 9%," she said with pride.

"Good. What is the cost of equity?"

"It is the dividends paid to the owners plus their expectation of growth in their investment as the company grows."

"My cost of equity is 40%, assuming your theoretical assumptions regarding my compensation."

"What is WACC?"

"It is the weighted average cost of financing the company."

"What is your WACC?"

"Once again, based on your theoretical numbers, it would be 27.6%."

"Wow."

She smiled with great pride and looked absolutely amazing. Her eyes seemed to sparkle with the satisfaction she felt in her success at being quizzed. The attendant was back again with another service and so they took another break from the numbers. "I have a proposal," he said.

"What is that?" she responded with one eyebrow raised.

"I don't know your name, where you are from, if you are married or otherwise involved. I don't even really know where you are going other than a purchasing trip with a flight landing in Paris. Let's assume that none of that matters. We will share this flight and this discussion. We will enjoy this moment and never see each other again."

She wrinkled her brow at the strange suggestion and then after a quick reflection said, "That is a wonderful idea." He suspected that in the back of her mind it was her intent anyway, but he had actually put it into words.

He continued, "You see, with no potential for any follow-up or other connection, we can enjoy a bad blind date without regard to any baggage."

"Are you saying I would be a bad blind-date?"

"Not at all, I just remember a girl much like you who was physically attractive and very popular who ended up as my date in high school. I knew that she wondered how she ever got stuck with me. She did not have the capability to celebrate an evening with someone very different from herself, explore the adventure of a unique opportunity and leave it at that. It turned out to be a very difficult evening."

She seemed to accept his explanation. After dinner most of the people around them were settling into the movie that was provided or just sleeping. "Are we getting any closer?" she asked.

"I still think Paris is several hours away."

"No, I was referring to the illusive GBER."

"Oh. Well, the next thing we need to do is investigate Break-Even Analysis," he instructed.

"I'm ready," she offered with encouragement.

A Little Short

"Most companies use Break-Even analysis to look at the operations of a department or operating unit. I think it can be used for a more global view. The problem with classical Break-Even is that it ends up determining how many units should be produced so that the revenues exactly equal the expenses. In that case the units have to be homogeneous or all the same. Things get really muddy when a department has multiple types of products at varying costs or prices."

"That sounds relatively restrictive. I have one store, and it has various departments, but even in each department we sell so many different priced goods that it sounds as if Break-Even has no applicability."

"I have determined the easiest way to equate everything on a relative scale is to talk in terms of price and total revenue instead of total units. So I try to determine the revenue that would be required to Break-Even and not the number of units."

"Will total revenue take care of all the differences?" she questions.

"Not all of them and it is still somewhat imperfect, but it is the best for a quick analysis."

"I can accept that, but you know---it doesn't cost me any more to sell a very expensive item than an inexpensive one. As a result, I would think mix becomes a fairly critical thing."

"You are jumping ahead of me, but that is good, it just shows that you are becoming invested in the analysis."

"Well, this is my business, and my life," she admitted.

"The next thing we need to focus on is costs. Remember the income statement we summarized:

Before			After
Revenue	$5,000	$5,000	Revenue
Oper Exp	($4,682)	($4,482)	Oper Exp
Depr. Exp	($125)	($125)	Depr Exp
EBIT	193	393	EBIT
Int Exp	($60)		
EBT	133	393	EBT
Taxes	($33)	($98)	Taxes
Net Inc	$100	$295	NOPAT

"I have consolidated all other operating costs into the 'Operating Expenses' category except for depreciation, interest, and taxes. We need to break these Operating Expenses out into their fixed and variable components."

"What do you mean fixed and variable?"

Fixed and Variable
He continued, "Bear with me for a moment here. I thought I saw some quarterly statements in your folder." He flipped through the pages. "Here they are. I'm going to summarize only the quarterly numbers for revenue and operating expenses for each quarter." He listed on a paper the following:

	1st Q	2nd Q	3rd Q	4th Q
Revenue	800	1,200	1,300	1,700
Oper Exp	900	1,050	1,180	1,352

"The Operating Expense excludes the excess salaries, depreciation expense, interest expense and taxes. If I add it up it will total $4,482, which agrees with our revised Income Statement. It appears that your sales are increasing and somewhat seasonal."

"That's right. Our biggest quarter is always the fourth quarter and our weakest is the first. Even at that we are seeing continued growth in sales, year over year. I'm still wondering about this fixed versus variable," she added.

"Over a short period which we call the relevant range, some of your costs will remain the same irrespective of the level of sales. Other costs will go up and down as revenue moves up or down. Over a short period of time we try to find how much will fit into either category. Over a longer period of time, say several years, you may convert some of the fixed to variable and some of the variable to fixed costs."

"What do you mean?"

"Let's talk about salaries. Fixed costs would be anyone who is paid a fixed monthly salary regardless of the level of sales. Variable costs would be commissions that are paid as a result of the level of sales. These are pure examples. There could also be salaries for some people that are mixed and have some fixed and variable elements."

"It sounds like a difficult problem trying to separate the two."

"It certainly can be. If you were to look at your list of operating costs and expenses--- cost-of-goods-sold, salaries and wages, employee benefits, rent, utilities, supplies, advertising; insurance, licenses, sales taxes, professional fees, and other---it could be an overwhelming task to estimate how much of each was fixed and how much was variable."

"Absolutely," she admitted.

"There are easier ways to do this. Now that we have some data over time, such as the quarterly operating revenue and expense numbers, we can simply feed them into a program that can automatically calculate the fixed and variable for us. This will be pretty crude because for a statistical model like this to work with a fair degree of reliability we would need about thirty observations instead of just four. Even though this is pretty rough, it will give us some idea."

He unbuckled his seat belt, stood up in the aisle, opened the overhead compartment and began searching for his laptop. Once he found it, he returned to his seat and turned it on. "I'm going to access a spreadsheet program and enter the quarterly numbers. Now I can highlight the data I want to analyze and ask the computer to graph the data with revenue across the bottom and expenses up the left hand side. Once these points are plotted I can ask the computer to fit a straight trend line through the points. The line may not go exactly through every point, but it does the best job it can. Then I ask the computer to give me a formula for the line and how well the data fits."

She leaned in close and studied what he was doing. Being a typical number cruncher he was more aware of the work he was doing than the closeness she offered. He highlighted the data that he wanted to use and clicked on an icon that translated the information into a graph. He then clicked on another menu item and a line appeared that ran relatively close to the four dots on the graph, followed by two formulas. The following image showed the results:

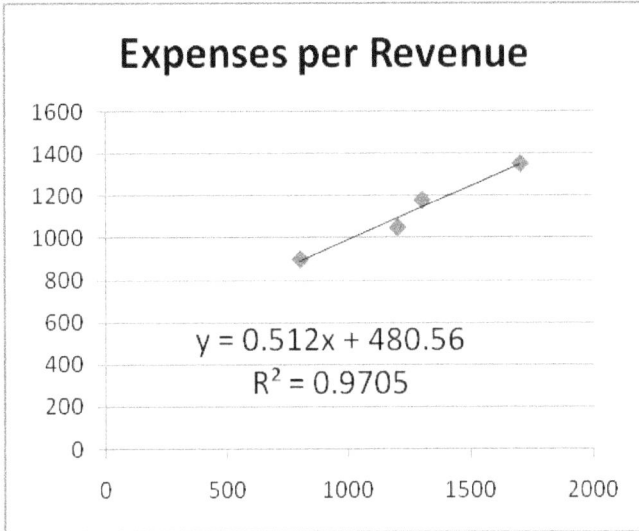

Expenses per Revenue

$$y = 0.512x + 480.56$$
$$R^2 = 0.9705$$

"Isn't that nice," he said with satisfaction.

"I recall something about this from a couple of my business courses, but it still makes very little sense."

"That's okay. You don't need to know everything about the process or how to even build it. What you do need to know is what it tells us."

"And what is that?"

"See the formula: **y = 0.512x + 480.56**?"

"Yes."

"The y is the level of operating expense that will result from some level of revenue. It will go up or down as revenue changes, based on the formula. The x is the revenue. As the revenue changes, it will dictate a specific expense level to match the sales. The 480.56 is the level of fixed costs or expenses. Regardless of the level of revenue there will be $480,560 in expenses every quarter over a relevant range. So from this you know that every quarter you will have at least that much in costs and expenses."

As he continued his explanation he noticed her long dark hair fall over his arm next to the computer. Was he being deceptive to enjoy the closeness of this beautiful creature under the pretext of explaining Break-Even?

"What does the 0.512 represent?" she asked.

"That is the variable cost piece. For every dollar in revenue you will incur 51.2 cents in costs. If you sell $1,000,000 in a month, you can expect variable costs to be 51.2% of that or $512,000. Theoretically, if in some quarter you sold nothing you would have zero variable costs but $480,560 in fixed costs and be losing money. On the other hand if you had revenue of $2,000,000 in a quarter you would have $480,560 in fixed costs and---let's see." He quickly multiplied $2,000,000 by .512. "And $1,024,000 in variable costs. Your total costs would be $1,504,560 and you would make money."

Rev	$ 2,000,000	
Var %	51.2%	
Var Cost		$ 1,024,000
Fixed Cost		$ 480,560
Tot Cost		$ 1,504,560

"How does it help me to know this?" she asked.

"If you are operating in the red, then you might want to consider converting some of your fixed costs to variable. If you are operating in the black it could be better to go the other direction and make some of your variable costs more fixed."

"How do I do that?"

"Some leases can be structured with more fixed than variable or more variable than fixed. Employees can be put on salary or straight commission. This can help management on both the downside and the upside."

"Interesting," she mused as she pulled back and studied him. "Okay, some costs are fixed and some are variable, where do we go from here?"

Catching some BERs

"Most educational programs that teach Break-Even use a model where fixed costs are divided by the contribution margin percentage to arrive at the required revenue."

"Wait a minute. What is contribution margin percentage? I don't recall talking about that."

"The contribution margin is the reciprocal or compliment of the variable cost. For every dollar of revenue you have 51.2 cents or 51.2 percent in variable costs. All the rest of the revenue, above and beyond variable costs, contributes to paying for the fixed costs. In your case it would be $1.00 minus .512 or .488 cents. This can also be stated in percentage terms as 48.8% of revenue goes to covering fixed costs. Classical Break-Even probably includes all operating costs, depreciation, interest and excess salaries as fixed costs in the calculation. I have specifically excluded all three in this application."

"What about taxes?"

"Since we are talking about Break-Even there would be no taxes as the result of no profit."

"Okay," she agreed.

"Because I have excluded depreciation, interest and excess salaries, I call the resulting revenue that is calculated CBER or the Cash

Break-Even Revenue. You could operate at this level if you were in a bind and didn't have cash to reinvest in assets or pay for your financing costs. This is a very short-term Break-Even."

"What does that mean for me?"

"Let's try it. Fixed costs of $480,560 divided by 48.8 percent gives us $984,754. Now, that is a quarterly number so we would have to multiply it by four to get the total year's cash Break-Even revenue of $3,939,016.

Cash Break-Even Revenue

	Amount	%
Revenue	3,939,016	100.0%
Variable Costs	(2,016,776)	51.2%
Cont. Margin	1,922,240	48.8%
Fixed Costs	(1,922,240)	
Depreciation Exp.	-	
E.B.I.T.	(0)	

"I made about $5,000,000 last year," she pointed out.

"So you were above your Cash Break-Even Revenue, but now we need to look at your OBER or your Operating Break-Even Revenue."

Typical (OBER)

"OBER, oh yes, I forgot about my good friend OBER," she said facetiously.

"To get to OBER we simply add depreciation to the fixed cost, $480,560 times four gets us to an annual fixed cost of $1,922,240, plus depreciation expense of $125,000 for a total fixed of $2,047,240. We divide that number by the contribution margin of 48.8 percent and get $4,195,164. That is your Operating Break-Even Revenue. At that revenue level you will cover all your operating costs."

Operating Break-Even Revenue

	Amount	%
Revenue	4,195,164	100.0%
Variable Costs	(2,147,924)	51.2%
Cont. Margin	2,047,240	48.8%
Fixed Costs	(1,922,240)	
Depreciation Exp.	(125,000)	
E.B.I.T.	0	

"I'm still ahead of that one."

"That's good."

"So far I'm looking like a pretty good business woman, at least when you crunch the numbers.

"So far so good," he agreed.

Looking up he noticed a fellow standing by the lavatory door a few rows ahead. That certainly seemed like a good idea and so he excused himself, got up and went to stand in line and wait his turn.

The fellow in front of him casually turned and said: "Now don't take this wrong, but from appearances, I never would have put you two together, but based on your interaction, you are obviously a couple. You are a lucky guy."

Just then the restroom door opened, a passenger came out and the fellow who had been making the observations went in. As the door closed and locked, he looked down to examine his boring attire and then glanced back at the woman he had been conversing with. She was pretty impressive.

The irony of the situation almost made him chuckle. Appearances can definitely send a message that can be quite different than reality. She was a beautifully intimidating woman that he found confident and approachable. Their intense conversation may have given the impression to others they were a couple, but in fact they were total strangers who had no intention of anything more.

When he had retaken his seat, the boutique owner leaned over and asked if he was ready to continue. He nodded.

"Okay, we have CBER and OBER, is it time for GBER?" she asked.

"I think so," he offered.

The Big One (GBER)

He explained, "CBER tells us if we are covering all our operating cash costs and can survive for a short-period of time. OBER tells us if we are covering all of our operating costs, including depreciation expense. GBER, the Global Break-Even Revenue, will tell us if we are covering all our operating and financing costs and if we are maintaining value in our business."

"So this is the big one?"

"That's right. In each case, CBER, OBER and GBER, we divide fixed costs by the contribution margin or 48.8%. The trick is in defining what our fixed costs are. All we used for CBER were fixed cash operating expenses. For OBER we used all fixed operating expenses, which included depreciation. For GBER we add all of the financing costs to the fixed operating costs."

He continued, "In the first two situations there were no taxes involved, but when it comes to financing costs we must consider taxes because we will have to pay some to get to a point where there is no residual income. Financing Costs will be calculated by multiplying the WACC which was what?"

She quickly looked at the scribbling on the papers in front of them. "It is 27.6%."

"We multiply that percentage by the total Financing Capital which is?"

Once again she searched the numbers in front of them. "I can't find it."

"It is the total of Notes Payable and Equity on the Balance Sheet."

"That's right. It is $1,250,000."

"So, a WACC of 27.6% times total Financing Capital of $1,250,000 results in $345,000 which I call the capital charge."

$$27.6\% \times \$1,250,000 = \$345,000$$

"Unfortunately, that is an after-tax number and so I need to know how much to earn to cover both taxes and the capital charge."

"I thought you said there were no taxes in Break-Even," she complained.

"Technically, that is right, but when it comes to financing costs and WACC these are after-tax numbers and so a company would need to provide for taxes."

"Okay, if you say so," she conceded.

"To find the before tax amount we know that taxes represent 25% of the before tax number leaving 75% after taxes. Dividing the $345,000 by 75%, that it represents, we get $460,000 as the before tax number.

$$\frac{\$\ 345,000}{75\%} = \$460,000$$

"That is the amount that is added to all fixed operating costs. Do you recall what fixed operating costs we used for the OBER calculation?"

She looked through the calculations again and said, "Here it is, $2,047,240."

Global Break-Even Revenue

	Amount	%
Revenue	5,137,787	100.0%
Variable Costs	(2,630,547)	51.2%
Cont. Margin	2,507,240	48.8%
Fixed Costs	(2,382,240)	
Depreciation Exp.	(125,000)	
E.B.I.T.	460,000	100.0%
Taxes	115,000	25.0%
NOPAT	345,000	75.0%
Capital Charge	(345,000)	
Residual Income	(0)	

"I add $460,000 to $2,047,240 and get $2,507,240 as my numerator. Dividing that number by my contribution margin of 48.8%, gives me $5,137,787."

"And what is that?"

"That is your GBER."

"Is that good or bad?"

"You had total revenue of $5,000,000 as compared to a GBER of $5,137,787. This would mean that you are not covering all your operating, financing, and tax costs. You were in the black on your earnings and even NOPAT looked to be a pretty robust number, but in reality with a very aggressive growth expectation, you are not yet where you need to be. Let's recast the GBER format with your $5,000,000 revenue"

Global Break-Even Revenue

	Amount	%
Revenue	5,000,000	100.0%
Variable Costs	(2,560,000)	51.2%
Cont. Margin	2,440,000	48.8%
Fixed Costs	(1,922,240)	
Depreciation Exp.	(125,000)	
E.B.I.T.	392,760	100.0%
Taxes	98,190	25.0%
NOPAT	294,570	75.0%
Capital Charge	(345,000)	
Residual Income	(50,430)	

"Your residual income is a negative $50,430.

"I'm a little stunned," she admitted.

"A lot of companies are in the same boat. They just don't realize the full cost of equity and in particular the impact that growth has on capital needs. Now if you were above GBER then you would be adding value to the business, but as it is, you are consuming value."

"What do you mean adding or consuming value? My clients receive great value from me. My clothes and accessories are of the highest quality and the women who purchase them and wear them are richer for it."

"I don't question that, but as a company you are not worth what has been invested in it."

"I'm confused."

"Well, if I was going to buy your company, I wouldn't pay more than book value and perhaps not even that much."

"What is book value and what do you mean?"

"If I subtract the $500,000 loan from your Financing Capital, I end up with $750,000. That is the book value of your equity. If I was going to buy your business right now I'm not sure I would pay more than that to acquire your equity. Of course this gets into a whole other discussion of what I call VIBE or the Value in Break-Even."

Just then the attendant announced that the lights would be going down so people could sleep on this overnight flight.

Feel the Vibe

When he awoke, he looked over to see
her curled up, her head resting on a flight pillow
and a flight blanket covering her body. The
light was streaming through a couple of
windows whose shades had been raised. The
other passengers were in various stages of sleep
and partial awareness. A few were wandering
the aisles and stretching their legs.

He sensed it was time for another visit to
the restroom so he got up and went to the door.
The small sliding sign said "Occupied," so he
leaned against the bulkhead waiting his turn.

When he had gained access and found
the relief the lavatory provided he opened the
door to see her standing there, waiting to be
next to use the facility. He sized her up to be
about five foot five, several inches shorter than
he was. "Good morning," he greeted her.

She nodded acknowledgment, let him
pass, entered the facility, and closed the door.
He returned to his seat just as the lights were
activated, illuminating the whole area.

When she returned, he got up to let her
slide past him and then settled down again. She
didn't appear to be a morning person; she was
quiet and withdrawn.

The attendant was upon him with pre-
breakfast service. He washed his hands with the

hot hand towel and curiously watched the others around him.

They sat in silence eating their breakfast as he explored the offerings on the TV screen embedded in the back of the seat in front of him.

When the breakfast trays were taken away and as he nursed a cup of coffee, he heard, "How did you sleep?" He turned, and she seemed to have come back to life.

"Not very well," he said, "and you?"

"Surprisingly well," she responded.

He assumed their discussion of the previous night was concluded until she spoke up. "Were you going to tell me something about the value of my business and some term you referred to as Vibe?"

"It gets more complicated. We would need to do some projections of next year's revenue and how that translates into NOPAT. We would need to estimate short-term and long-term growth rates, in addition to any adjustments in WACC, Fixed Costs and Variable Costs. The bottom line is this---the more your residual income grows the more the market value will exceed book value."

"What is residual income?"

"Remember, that is the excess above and beyond GBER. Some people call it residual income, some call it excess earnings and others refer to it as EVA or Economic Value Added.

They are all very similar. There is a direct correlation with the value a company is creating and that excess."

"I feel very strongly that revenues will grow by at least 20% per year over the next several years."

She seemed to want to explore the issue and so he pulled out his pad of paper and began making notes.

"I'm going to make some pencil scratching to see what kind of a value we could place on your boutique. These are my assumptions. Next year's revenue will be 20% higher than this year or $6,000,000. We will keep variable costs at 51.2% of revenue so that contribution margin will remain at 48.8%. What do you think fixed costs will do?" he asked.

"I'm not sure what is included in fixed costs. If it is as you say, those costs that remain unchanged from month to month without regard to a change in the level of sales, there may be more change than just inflation. If I have a 20% increase in sales, I will probably have to bring on a couple more salaried employees. I've also been thinking of doubling my monthly advertising budget."

"What do you think the impact of those two changes will be?"

She thought for a moment. "I think it would work out to be at least another hundred grand."

"Let's see, last year's fixed cost was $480,560 per quarter or $1,922,240. If we raise that by an inflation rate of say 3%, it will go up to $1,979,907. If we add $100,000 for the changes you have identified, then next year's fixed costs would be about $2,079,907. If we increase depreciation expense slightly, by 3% to cover increased assets from the prior year's acquisitions, that will add another $3,750. That will leave us with $719,343 EBIT."

Global Break-Even Revenue

	Amount	%
Revenue	6,000,000	100.0%
Variable Costs	(3,072,000)	51.2%
Cont. Margin	2,928,000	48.8%
Fixed Costs	(2,079,907)	
Depreciation Exp.	(128,750)	
E.B.I.T.	719,343	100.0%
Taxes (25%)	179,836	25.0%
NOPAT	539,507	75.0%

"What was that you said?"

"EBIT---that is short for Earnings Before Interest and Taxes. It is your operating earnings before the application of taxes. Of course it excludes interest expense. You paid 25% tax in the year just finished. Will that rate continue?"

"I don't know. My accountant was able to take advantage of some special deductions that reduced the rate. I'm not sure what that rate will be in the future."

"Well, let's just keep it there for now at 25% for taxes. So with taxes of $179,836 we will end up with $539,507 NOPAT."

"It looks like that is about double the previous year," she said with pride.

"Not bad. We now need to consider what will happen to the balance sheet when revenues increase by 20%. If you continue your credit policies with your customers and your vendors and if you maintain the same proportional level of inventory on hand, then your operating capital will need to grow by 20% in line with the change in revenue. Do you have enough capacity with your existing property, plant and equipment to support a 20% growth in revenue without buying more registers, display racks, computers, and things like that?"

"There are always things that come up. My assistant in accessories sees a huge upside potential for her area. She has done very well so far, but I'm nervous about the kind of expansion she is proposing."

"What does she want to do?"

"There is some unused space in the back of the next shop that we could acquire and expand into. It would require knocking out a wall and remodeling the area. I do really great when it comes to clothing, but I know my limits and accessories are my weak spot. She has been terrific in the past with a great eye for what will sell, but I just went through the expansion into the discount space down the street. I don't know how aggressive to be."

"How loyal is she?"

"What do you mean?"

"If she is really good, how long can you keep her? Can she make more somewhere else or even open her own shop? Can she be replaced easily?"

"Those are all great questions that I don't have an answer for right now," she admitted.

"Would it be safe to say that you will need some expansion of your fixed assets to support the growth you're talking about?

"Undoubtedly," she confirmed.

"Let's factor in a 15% increase in total assets for the coming year. That covers the 20% increase in operating assets and something for a change in fixed assets or property, plant and equipment."

"Fair enough," she said.

"Total assets were $1,550,000 last year. Subtracting current liabilities of $300,000 from current assets of $925,000 will give us $625,000 of net operating capital. Adding fixed assets of $1,000,000, less $375,000 of accumulated depreciation, results in $1,250,000 of Net Operating and Invested Capital. That exactly equals our Financing Capital.

Balance Sheet
(Change)

	This Yr	chng	Next Yr
Cash & Cash Equiv	150	30	180
Accounts Receivable	325	65	390
Inventory	300	60	360
Other Current Assets	150	30	180
Current Assets	925	185	1,110
Accounts Payable	(250)	(50)	(300)
Other Cur. Liab.	(50)	(10)	(60)
Net Oper Capital	625	125	750
Prop, Plant & Equip	1,000	191	1,191
Accumulated Deprec	(375)	(129)	(504)
Oper & Inv Cap	1,250	187	1,437

Notes Payable	500		500
Total Debt	800		500
Common Stock	700		700
Retained Earnings	50	187	237
Financing Cap	1,250	187	1,437

"If Net Operating Capital changes by 20% we get $750,000. Assuming depreciation expense goes up a little to $129,000 and the overall change in Financing Capital is 15% then Property, plant and equipment would go up by $191,000."

"Multiplying that number by the WACC of 27.6% we get $396,474 for our capital charge.

$$27.6\% \quad \times \quad \$1,436,500 \quad = \quad \$396,474$$

Let's add that to the worksheet:

Global Break-Even Revenue

	Amount	%
Revenue	6,000,000	100.0%
Variable Costs	(3,072,000)	51.2%
Cont. Margin	2,928,000	48.8%
Fixed Costs	(2,079,907)	
Depreciation Exp.	(128,750)	
E.B.I.T.	719,343	100.0%
Taxes (25%)	179,836	25.0%
NOPAT	539,507	75.0%
Capital Charge	(396,474)	
Residual Income	143,033	

That will leave a residual income of $143,033 which is a significant improvement over the Break-Even of the previous year."

"That's fine. I think we are going to be in great shape. So how does that translate into the value of the boutique?"

Residual Income Value
    "The theory is that if you are at Break-Even, with a zero residual income, then the value of the company is equal to the book value of your financing capital. Value is added by dividing the projected residual income by a capitalization factor. That factor is the difference between the WACC and your projected long-term growth rate. Although the estimates for each are important, the most critical thing is the difference between them."
    "I'm not sure I'm following you."
    "I know it sounds complicated. Let me just say the difference is seldom below 3% and usually higher. In your case, with a 27.6% WACC or what we call the discount rate we need to find the long-term growth assumption. In the next few years you may grow at 20% per year, but that rate is difficult to sustain over a long period of time. The growth rate for most companies eventually moves to the average nominal rate of increase for the economy as a whole. That would be around 6%, which would include 3% for inflation and 3% for increased productivity."
    "If we average the short-term rate of 20% and the longer-term rate of 6% we get

around a 13% overall rate. Subtracting that rate from 27.6% would result in a difference of 14.6%. Dividing $143,033 residual income by the 14.6%, results in a $979,678 in value to add to the book value of $1,436,500. The total value of the financing capital would be 2,416,178."

$$\frac{\$ \ 143,033}{14.6\%} = \$979,678$$

$$\$979,678 \ + \ \$1,436,500 \ = \ \$2,416,178$$

Rule of Thumb Value

"I'm not sure that is very realistic. On the other hand, a recent study has shown that small companies like yours usually sell for about two times next year's projected earnings. If I use NOPAT as an earnings proxy I would get a price of two times $539,507 or $1,079,014. That would be a rule of thumb."

$$2 \ \times \ \$539.507 \ = \ \$1,079,014$$

"Those are extreme differences."
"They really are. I think the smaller the company, the closer to the minimum price of $1,079,014. The larger the company the closer the price would be to the maximum of $2,416,178. We would need to do a lot more work to nail down a good number."

Free Cash Flow Value

"One other approach to finding value is the free cash flow method. In this calculation we subtract the change in your operating and investing capital of $187,500 from your NOPAT of $537,507 and get $352,007."

$$\$537,507 \ - \ \$187,500 \ = \ \$352,007$$

"We call that your free cash flow to investors. If we divide that number by the difference between your WACC and long-term growth of 14.6% we get $2,411,007 for a value."

$$\frac{\$ \ 352,007}{14.6\%} = \$2,411,007$$

"Wow, that seems really close to the number you got for a maximum you calculated using the residual income," she noticed.

"Great observation, both calculations started with NOPAT and utilized WACC and the long-term growth rate. One factored in the change in the financing capital and the other the charge on financing capital. These are all really quick and dirty calculations, but let's just say that you will be adding value to your company above and beyond its book value as you continually see positive residual values in the future. What do you think?" he asked.

"My sense is that you aren't simply giving me a freebie here, but setting me up for a follow-up consulting engagement," she questioned.

"Remember our agreement---no names, no strings, and no follow-up. Let's just celebrate the moment and leave it at that," he responded. He decided to pull back a little now and not go into all the specifics of a more precise valuation for her. It appeared she could sense this and didn't press the issue. They both pulled away.

As she settled back into her seat and examined all the numbers just presented, he unzipped his GBER-marked executive case and began pouring over the presentation he was about to give, while she reviewed more data from her business. Occasionally they offered a passing comment to each other, but he realized nothing would come from this and it was basically over.

The plane touched down and everyone anxiously waited for the outer door to open and spill passengers onto the jet way and into the terminal. Finally, the seatbelt light went off and everyone stood up. He focused on extracting his carryon from the overhead bin and working his way to the passageway.

As he walked along, he felt a slight tug on his shirt-sleeve and turned to see her walking beside him. She leaned toward him and said, "I will be having dinner alone tonight on the Bateaux Dinner Cruise that leaves the terminal directly across from the Eiffel Tower at 9 pm. I think it is a real shame to have to eat alone."

This caught him off guard and he slowed his walk to contemplate what she had said. As he did, she moved past him, glanced back, offered him a confident smile and was off, lost in the crowd.

Am I Seine?

He stood high up on the Eiffel Tower and looked down at the Seine. He could see the bridge and the boat dock next to it. He looked at his watch; it was 8:30 pm. He wondered what might be waiting for him at that boat dock. Was she jesting or not?

As he slowly approached the dock, he scanned the crowd waiting there. It was a beautiful evening. The water danced and reflected the lights of the boats and the street lamps. He glanced in the direction of the Champs-Elysees and the lights of the city.

He rounded the corner, still uncertain that she would be there and if she was, could he find her? Did he really want to find her?

"There you are," he heard. He turned and saw her standing about fifteen feet away. She was wearing a simple white sleeveless dress with a scooped neckline and a dark accent belt. As she moved toward him the white fabric flowed with the motion of her body.

"What am I doing?" he thought to himself.

She approached him, smiled and putting her left arm through his, she motioned with her right arm toward the waiting boat. They descended the stairs and he felt a soft breeze off the water. Again, the thought echoed in his mind, "What am I doing?"

They were directed toward the front of the boat and a prime table. From here they could see everything. "Did you present today?" she asked.

"No, it's tomorrow at 10:00 am."

"I'm not going to ask if you have been to Paris before or what you did today. I love it when you talk about my business. You get so excited, and as crazy as it sounds, I find it really compelling and revealing."

Thoughts quickly shot through his head. Sure, on the flight the whole conversation was about her. He knew she was going to be disappointed with a follow-up without the confinement and protection of the plane, but wait---what did he care? She meant nothing to him and she was sucking him into her intimidating power again. "Okay, you asked for it, we are going to talk ethics."

"What do you mean?"

"You know, right and wrong---stuff like that."

It appeared that this wasn't exactly what she had in mind. After a pause she concluded, "You are full of surprises."

He had seized the moment and taken her completely off guard. "I have a total portrait of you except for what your ethical and moral standards are."

The boat was moving and Paris was indeed the city of lights with illuminated buildings passing by on both sides. A waiter began the food service as a bridge passed overhead.

He looked over to see young couples on the broad walkway along the Seine. Some were holding hands and some locked in an embrace. Here he was with one of the most beautiful women he had ever met and in one of the most romantic settings, and he was going to talk about ethics! He braced himself and committed to resist being seduced by the elements around him.

Me, We, or Thee

"I have a theory about ethics," he offered.

"Yes, and what is that?" she responded, raising one eyebrow.

"I call it Me, We, or Thee. Are our actions influenced more by our own personal will, by family, friends and fraternal associations, or by science, sage or scripture?"

"I've never heard such a thing."

"Let me pose a couple of moral dilemmas and you tell me how you would respond."

"Okay."

"What do you do with unwanted customers, people who come to your shop that you would rather not serve?"

She was taken aback. "You go right for the jugular. Here let me claw you away from my neck." She motioned as though to tear his hand from that beautiful pedestal on which her flawless head rested.

"Well, what do you do?" he pressed.

Unwanted Customers

"There are people who come to the shop that simply shouldn't be there. They are dressed inappropriately and would detract from the image we are trying to project, or they obviously don't have the resources and could occupy a great deal of our time without making the sale."

"So how do you deal with it?"

"We certainly don't ignore the problem but instead confront it head on. We efficiently assess the situation, greet the person, determine their needs and try to direct them to the appropriate place where there needs can best be fulfilled. We occasionally suggest, with great care and tact that they might find exactly what they are looking for at a store across the street.

"How did you arrive at that solution? Did you initiate it from your own wisdom, did you adopt it from what you observed peers were doing, or is there some industry sage who you look to for advice on such issues?"

"I think it came from my previous employers where I learned how to run a store."

Stealing Customer

"Okay, next situation, how would you handle a rich celebrity who was caught taking things without paying for them?"

"You are cruel and go right to the heart of the matter," she said, putting her clasped hands to the middle of her chest, emphasizing her breasts.

He was trying to remain on a very high business level and an ethical one at that, and every action she offered drew him back to her sensuality.

She thought for a moment. "We had a situation like this and it was probably one of the most difficult things I've ever had to deal with. Even though we caught this woman red handed outside the store with items she had not paid for in her bag, it was still her word against ours."

"The first time we observed her on our hidden camera, the items were not very expensive and we wrote it off. The second time is when we caught her outside the store."

"Do you believe in punishment or grace?" he asked.

"I would like to say grace with some latitude, but for chronic offenders, you have to initiate tough love. You love them, but you are tough. We let her know we were aware of her actions and promised to prosecute if it ever happened again."

"Where did that policy come from? Did you unilaterally come up with it, did it come from your prior experience, or is it based on some sage, scientific study or scriptural doctrine?"

"I think mostly from my previous employment, but it could be a merging of all of the above."

Just then they looked up to see another bridge pass overhead and the magnificent lights on the buildings around them which were in turn reflected on the water.

The Final Question

"Let's go with one last question," he proposed.

"That sounds great," she concluded.

"Where do we go from here?"

She sat back in her chair and her eyes looked deep into his. "You know a great deal more about me that I do about you. Neither of us knows if the other is involved with someone or even married. We don't even know each other's names. I'm not sure."

He looked away at the water and could see the lights illuminating the upcoming bridge.

She spoke up softly, "If someone were to try and find your lecture tomorrow, where would they go?"

He smiled.

Summary of Concepts

Accounts Payable: If I divide your daily sales of $5,500 into the $250,000 of accounts payable, it tells me that from the time you receive your goods it takes you about 45 days to pay the vendors. Page 17

Accounts Receivable: If I divide the $325,000 in accounts receivable by your sales per day, you have about 24 days of sales that are uncollected at any one time. Page 12

Accrual Accounting: Accrual accounting helps to smooth things out and reflects a matching of revenues earned and the expenses that generated those revenues. Page 7

Adding Value: A lot of companies are in the same boat. They just don't realize the full cost of equity and in particular the impact that growth has on capital needs. Now if you were above GBER then you would be adding value to the business, but as it is, you are consuming value. Page 57-58

After-Tax cost of Debt: If I count that $15,000 in tax savings because of the interest expense, then the true cost is $45,000 divided by $500,000 or about 9%. Page 29

Break-Even Formula: Most educational programs that teach Break-Even use a model where fixed costs are divided by the contribution margin percentage to arrive at the required revenue. Page 50

Break-Even: The theory is that if you are at Break-Even, with a zero residual income, then the value of the company is equal to the book value of your financing. Page 67

Capital Charge: So, a WACC of 27.6% times total Financing Capital of $1,250,000 is $345,000. I call this my capital charge. Page 55

Capital: Accountants like to categorize groups of items on the balance sheet as Operating, Investing, and Financing Capital. Page 23

Capitalization Rate: If we average the short-term rate of 20% and the longer-term rate of 6% we get around a 13% overall rate. Subtracting that rate from 27.6% would result in a difference of 14.6%. Page 67-68

Cash Break-Even Revenue: Because I have excluded depreciation, interest and excess salaries, I call the resulting revenue that is calculated CBER or the Cash Break-Even Revenue. Page 50-51

Contribution Margin Percent: The contribution margin is the reciprocal of the variable cost number. For every dollar of revenue you have 51.2 cents or 51.2 percent in variable costs. All the rest of the excess revenue contributes to paying for the fixed costs. In your case it would be $1.00 minus .512 or .488 cents. This can also be stated in percentage terms as 48.8% of revenue goes to covering fixed costs. Page 50

Extending Credit: She wanted to set up a revolving account and charge it. I saw this as a way to capture even more of her business and establish a permanent customer. Page 13

Financing Capital Structure Weights: Let's see---$500,000 of debt divided by $1,250,000 Financing Capital is 40% and $750,000 Equity divided by the same $1,250,000 is 60%. Page 36

Financing versus Operating: The decision regarding how much to borrow, is completely independent from the ongoing operations of the business. Page 24

Fixed and Variable Formula: The y is the operating expense level and the x is the revenue. As the revenue changes, it will dictate a specific expense level to match the sales. The

480.56 is the level of fixed costs. Regardless of the level of revenue there will be $480,560 in expenses every quarter over a relevant range. So from this you know that every quarter you will have at least that much in costs and expenses. Page 47-48

Free Cash Flow Value: "One other approach to finding value is the free cash flow method. In this calculation we subtract the change in your operating and investing capital of $187,500 from your NOPAT of $537,507 and get $352,007. We call that your free cash flow to investors. If we divide that number by the difference between your WACC and long-term growth of 14.6% we get $2,411,007 for a value." Page 69

Global Break-Even Revenue: That's right. In each case, CBER, OBER and GBER, we divide fixed costs by the contribution margin or 48.8%. The trick is in defining what our fixed costs are. All we used for CBER were fixed cash operating expenses. For OBER we used all fixed operating expenses, which included depreciation. For GBER we add all of the financing costs to the fixed operating costs. Page 54

Hidden Dividends: That's $200,000 (for management and buying) compared to the

$400,000 you are taking. The difference of $200,000 is really a dividend or a return on your equity investment as an owner. Page 30

Income Tax Rate: Taxes were $33,000, so if I add that back to the Net Income of $100,000, the before tax amount would be $133,000. It looks like the tax rate was about 25%, or $33,000 taxes on $133,000 of before-tax income. Page 25

Interest Expense: If we didn't have the interest expense, then the income tax would be much higher. We say that interest expense provides a tax break. Page 24

Inventory: Dividing the $300,000 inventory by the $5,500 in the cost of daily sales indicates that an item will remain on the racks for almost 55 days before it goes out the door. Page 14

Me, We, or Thee: I call it Me, We, or Thee. Are our actions influenced more by our own personal will, by family, friends and fraternal associations, or by science, sage or scripture? Page 74

Net Income versus NOPAT: Instead of $100,000 of Net Income, we now have $145,000 NOPAT or Net Operating Profit After-Taxes. Page 26

Net Income versus NOPAT: That is true. If we look at the newly adjusted NOPAT of $295,000 we find three things there: $100,000 of original Net Income, $150,000 of net dividends to equity holders and $45,000 of net interest expense. The first two belong to the equity investors, it's just that $100,000 is reinvested back into the company on the equity holder's behalf and the $150,000 is paid out as a dividend. Page 32

Operating Break-Even Revenue: To get to OBER we simply add depreciation to your fixed cost, $480,560 times four gets us to an annual fixed cost of $1,922,240, plus depreciation expense of $125,000 for a total fixed of $2,047,240. We divide that number by the contribution margin of 48.8 percent and get $4,195,164. That is your operating Break-Even revenue. Page 52

Power Trio: The two operating assets we just discussed, accounts receivable and inventory, plus one of your operating liabilities, accounts payable, I refer to as the power trio. Page 16

Relevant Range: Over a short period which we call the relevant range, some of your costs will remain the same irrespective of the level of sales. Other costs will go up and down as revenue moves up or down. Over a short period of time we try to find how much will fit into either category. Page 44-45

Residual Income Value: Dividing $143,033 residual income by the 14.6%, results in a $979,678 in value to add to the book value of $1,436,500. The total value of the financing capital would be 2,416,178. Page 67-68

Revenue versus Units: I have determined the easiest way to equate everything on a relative scale is to talk in terms of price and total revenue instead of total units. Page 42

Rule of Thumb: A recent study has shown that small companies like yours usually sell for about two times next year's projected earnings. If I use NOPAT as an earnings proxy I would get a price of two times $539,507 or $1,079,014. That would be a rule of thumb. Page 68

Variable Costs: That is the variable cost piece. For every dollar in revenue you will incur 51.2 cents in costs. Page 48

Weighted Average Cost of Capital: If we multiply the weight of debt times the after-tax cost of debt we get a component cost of 3.6%. Then if we multiply the weight of equity times the cost of equity we get a component cost of

19.8%. Adding these two components together we get a weighted average cost of 27.6%. Page 36